ONE LADY AT A TIME

by
John Benton

John Benton Books
127 South El Molino Avenue
Pasadena, California 91101
(626) 405-0950

ISBN -0- 9635411-0-2

Ted Engstrom
President Emeritus
World vision

"I have been impressed with the quality of the outreach and ministry of the Walter Hoving Home, under the loving guidance and direction of John and Elsie Benton. The young ladies in their care are ministered to with a deep sense of Christian compassion and love. It is a significant work, most worthy of our support."

Billy Graham
Billy Graham Evangellistic Association

"In times like these we can all thank God for places like the Walter Hoving Home. I've watched this effective New York ministry grow for the past 25 years, and it has my 100% support. Now in California...will also have the same opportunities to start over in these Christ-honoring homes. I urge you to pray for and give to this powerful ministry."

Dale Evans Rogers

"Praise the Lord for the Christian ministry of John and Elsie Benton of the Walter Hoving Home. Elsie and John are a veritable beacon light of Christian love, beaming warm understanding, healing, and transforming Christian Holy spirit power in countless lives of desperate young women who have lost their way. God bless you beautiful Bentons!"

Ruth Graham

"Never before have so many young people in our country become so disenchanted, so bored and burdened with life, that they fall easy prey to the various escapes being offered. They find out too late that escapes such as drugs, turn instead into traps from which few escape."

"The Walter Hoving Home...is a place where such a girl can find a warm, loving welcome. Receive solid, practical help, and most important of all, be introduced to the Lord Jesus Christ Who alone can forgive sins, give power to resist temptation and make life worth living."

Pat Boone

"In my visits to the Walter Hoving Home...I've literally seen Jesus in action.

"Year after year, girls with no hope and tragic pasts are literally swept off the dead end street...and given new lives and new personalities. They are nursed to health, given whole new vision of life and their own worth, and introduced to Jesus. The transformations are miraculous, and I'm grateful for the chance to participate in the on-going miracles at the Walter Hoving Home."

Charles W. Colson
Founder/Chairman
Prison Fellowship

"I have seen the Walter Hoving Home ministry first hand and I am an enthusiastic supporter. It is a good example of people of the Church obeying our Lord's command to reach out to those in need."

INTRODUCTION

This book is about winning and losing, faith and unbelief, life and death, joy and sorrow . . . what all of us face in real life.

For the past twenty-five years at the Walter Hoving Home, Elsie and I have gone through unbelievable experiences.

You will read how I almost get killed. By pimps! Even today, I have to be very alert as a minister on the streets. They're always lurking close by and believe me, they are killers. You will read about Joe Loco who almost got me.

It isn't all morbid though. One of the greatest miracles I ever experienced was a young lady who was terribly demon possessed. She heard voices and saw demons. You will read how out of that horrible condition she's become an outstanding Christian, who holds important government positions today in the state of Virginia.

But strangely enough, this is my biggest battle . . . Money! It just seems we never have enough money. What we get in, we spend on necessary needs. Then we start the cycle all over again.

At times, it seems as though we will be plunged into bankruptcy. And then, out of a very dark night comes light and the next day someone sends us a generous check to keep us going.

You will read how we have been really up against the wall, and yet, God has His special angels who have ministered to us when we were flat on our backs.

Even though I minister to ladies who are prostitutes on the street, I have probably been propositioned more than any man on the face of this earth. I have never stepped over the line of immorality and there's a reason for it. My wife. You will read about Elsie and the spectacular ministry God has given her with our ladies. She's got a heart that's bigger than the world, that reaches out to everybody. I mean, literally everybody.

I don't want to tell you the whole story in this introduction, but as a result of traveling through its pages with me you will experience the faithfulness of God in these difficult times. And I do pray this book will increase your faith in God for your own needs.

John Benton

ONE LADY AT A TIME
By John Benton

CHAPTER I
WAS I REALLY GOING TO GET KILLED?

One Saturday night there was a rally down on the Lower East Side of Manhattan and we took all our girls. David Wilkerson, the founder of Teen Challenge, was the speaker. I was assisting him so I sat on the platform during his message.

The back door of the auditorium swung open and there stood a man. When I saw him, I immediately recognized who he was — Joe Loco, one of the most notorious pimps in New York City. I had met him before.

Joe slowly scanned the audience. I knew who he was looking for: Becky.

Becky had just come into our Home. We had been up in the Bronx at a street meeting and during the invitation to receive Christ, Becky stepped forward. She was a drug addict and prostitute and really needed the Lord.

That same evening, she came back home with us and entered the program.

And now, down toward the front of the auditorium, sat Becky, listening intently to Dave's sermon. Right next to her was an empty seat and Joe spotted it.

As he walked down the aisle, I kept my eyes riveted on him. I could see he was full of anger.

Joe plopped himself down next to Becky, startling her. Joe reached over and grabbed her arm.

I couldn't hear what they were saying, but an argument was soon going full swing.

Their voices got louder. Dave stopped his message, put his hand over the microphone, and turned toward me. "John, go down there and tell that guy to shut up," he said.

I didn't want to tell Dave that Joe was a violent pimp. And I'm sure David Wilkerson, who wasn't afraid of pimps, couldn't have cared less.

So I walked off the platform and said to Joe, "Would you mind coming out to the foyer with me?"

My heart was in my throat, and I barely got the words out. I was so scared I was ready to pass out.

Much to my surprise, Joe got up and walked to the back with me.

When we got to the foyer, I tried my best to explain to Joe why Becky wanted to stay in the program. She had given her life to Christ and really wanted to change.

Meanwhile, Becky was concerned about me. She knew Joe was a killer. Becky thought she had better check on me. And when she walked into the foyer, Joe leaped at her. Becky lunged out of the way and Joe started running after her.

They kind of ran around in a circle. When Joe came in front of me, I can't describe what came over me. I wish I could say it was "holy anger," but there was nothing holy about it.

As soon as Joe got in front of me I grabbed his shirt and held it up under his chin.

I really wanted to wrestle him to the ground and punch my fist into his face because I hated pimps.

At that time I really hadn't become streetwise. To say the least, this certainly was not God's wisdom being applied to the situation.

Rather than hitting Joe in the mouth right then, I swung his body around and pushed him across the foyer, past the swinging doors, across the sidewalk and slammed him up against a car.

When that happened, Joe exploded. He reached for his back pocket. I found out later that he carried his switchblade or a loaded revolver in that pocket.

If Joe got his knife, he'd flick it open and slash me across the stomach and disembowel me; if it was a gun, he'd blow my brains out.

Thank God, the Lord was trying to overcome my foolishness and protect me. There was a big guy standing next to me. When he saw what Joe was planning to do, he grabbed Joe and pinned his hands to his sides.

Joe started screaming and swearing at me. After what seemed like an eternity, he said to the guy holding him, "Okay, I'm all right now."

This guy relaxed his hold on Joe and my heart started pounding like crazy again.

Would Joe shoot me or stab me?

But Joe turned and started walking away. Then he stopped and pointed his finger at me. He swore and said, "Reverend Benton, I'm gonna get you." I knew what he meant . . . some day he would kill me.

Joe disappeared around the corner. But I was left with that devastating thought. Would he really kill me?

Becky and I talked further about it. The more she told me about how violent Joe was the more scared I got. She said one time some guys drove by cussing at Joe. He opened fire on the car and they returned fire. He carried two bullets in his legs where they had tried to kill him.

The service had ended, and I was really subdued. I kept thinking about Joe. When was he going to kill me?

On the way back to the Home I didn't say much. I just couldn't get my mind off Joe.

I stopped going up to the Bronx for street meetings. I knew Joe was up there waiting for me. And I shuddered to think of getting my head blown off by Joe Loco on a dark street in the Bronx.

During these times there was intense prayer for my safety. Other people knew what had happened, and out of their sympathy for me, a number of them told me they were praying for me. But it didn't seem to help.

I personally went to the Lord and decided to have it out. I couldn't sleep any more. I secretly almost wished Joe would kill me and get it over with. The pain was unbearable.

But I found the cause of the problem. "Lord, what went wrong?" I asked.

And in this still small voice, He gently told me. "John, you lost your temper with Joe Loco and did not act like a Christian. Furthermore, you owe Joe an apology."

I quickly responded, "God, you know Joe's a pimp and a killer. He's out to murder me!"

I shall never forget what the Lord spoke to me. "Jesus also died for pimps."

Now that's a tough one to take. Whether you or I like it or not, Christ still loves pimps. I must confess I don't fully understand that, because of their violent ways. But the truth still remains, Christ died for everyone.

"Lord what should I do?" I asked.

The Holy Spirit spoke to me again and said, "You owe Joe an apology. You should go ask him to forgive you."

God and I argued. I reminded God again that Joe was going to kill me. I even told God what Becky had told me. He had killed people before, and he would kill me.

I know that as Christians, we are supposed to give our lives to the Lord, but when it came to something like this I wasn't quite so sure.

But I knew God was right. I finally said, "God, if it means I'm going to be a martyr, then I'll be a martyr!"

I went back to the Bronx to do some witnessing with my staff. My real purpose, though, was to find Joe.

My wife Elsie and I are a team on the streets

14

because she's very brave. In fact, she has no fear of anyone. She keeps looking for people to witness to, even in dangerous situations. I keep looking out for pimps and muggers! I guess I'm a chicken Christian.

But this night Elsie was home with our kids and I was alone. After parking the van, I went up Westchester Avenue asking people if they had seen Joe Loco. People on the street knew what was going on, and I was told "No, man. We haven't seen him around for a couple weeks."

"Oh good, he probably got killed," I thought.

As I think back, that certainly wasn't very Christian! It was still hard to get through my head that Christ had died for even Joe Loco.

I came back the next week, and the week after that. Each time I heard that Joe wasn't there, the better I felt. But I always had that nagging question lurking in the back of my mind, "Where is Joe Loco?"

About the third week we went back to the same area. A guy came walking down the street and I went up to him. "Have you seen Joe Loco?"

The answer shocked me. "Yeah, man, he's down in that tavern over there." It was my moment of truth. Joe was back in town, and I had to confront him.

The guy was pointing toward Fox and Westchester. Someone had spray painted a single word on the soot-blackened wall: TERROR. Boy, was that right!

My heart started racing again. I just couldn't take

the pressure. I turned and stumbled toward the van. Then the Holy Spirit spoke, "Go and ask Joe for forgiveness."

I took a deep breath to try to slow my heart down. It didn't do any good.

As I turned back to head toward that tavern, I knew I was going to get killed. And yet if I didn't go, I would never find peace.

Somehow I made it to the door of the tavern and peered inside. It was dark in there, and the music was blaring.

My eyes got used to the darkness and I spotted the bartender. He stood there, with his hands on his hips, glaring at me.

Sometimes people mistake me for a detective. I guess I was making this bartender nervous.

But I ignored him and glanced down the bar. There didn't seem to be anybody there.

And then I saw him. Joe Loco was sitting on a bar stool, slumped over the counter.

My knees were weak and I felt like passing out. As I slowly started in Joe's direction, I began to cry out in my heart, "Please God, oh God, please help me, help me."

And then I began to get horrible thoughts. Maybe God hadn't spoken to me after all. Maybe it had just been my own thoughts.

But I kept walking toward him.

I could tell by the look on Joe's face that he was high. His eyes were closed. I stopped beside him and tried to say something, but no sound came out of my mouth.

Then I reached over and put my hand on his shoulder.

Just then, Joe slowly turned his head and looked at me. Then his head jerked as he recognized me.

"Joe, before you do or say anything, I've come here to tell you something," I blurted out.

I knew what Joe was expecting. He probably thought I was going to grab him and throw him out of the bar, across the sidewalk and slam him against a car.

I stood there, motionless. Then I looked Joe straight in the eye and said, "Joe, would you please forgive me for the way I acted to you a few weeks ago. I did not act like a Christian. Would you forgive me?"

Joe's mouth fell open. This wasn't what he had expected at all.

It seemed like an eternity that Joe stared at me. I wanted to say something, but didn't know what to say. I had delivered God's message.

But I knew no matter what happened next, I was not going to grab Joe and do something foolish. The next move was up to him.

My eyes dropped to Joe's hands. If he went for his hip pocket, I knew it would be all over. There was no big guy standing next to me like the other time. And I knew I couldn't depend on the bartender.

Joe kept staring at me. Then he finally said, "Yeah, Reverend, I forgive you."

I cannot describe what happened next. It's as though a ten-ton block of granite had just been lifted off my shoulders. I felt like singing Handel's Messiah at the top of my voice. I felt like hugging Joe. I even wanted to hug the bartender.

Joe forgave me!

The Holy Spirit's presence was so strong at that moment. I said to Joe, "Joe, what Becky has received, you can receive too."

Then I hesitated. Maybe I shouldn't have brought up Becky's name. That was his girl.

But I didn't stop there. I went on to explain the plan of salvation to Joe. I could sense an overwhelming presence of the Holy Spirit. Joe was really listening.

After I got through explaining to him how to receive Christ, I asked Joe, "Would you like to receive him as your personal Savior?"

The setting was certainly not a church — it was a bar and in the ghetto at that, with loud screaming music.

Joe fixed his gaze on me. He blinked a couple

times. "Yeah, I would."

I led Joe in the sinner's prayer. Then I prayed for him. As soon as I began praying, it was as though heaven had opened up and a flood fell upon us. The more I prayed, the more I cried.

Then I heard Joe. He was weeping. His shoulders were heaving up and down.

This tavern, in the middle of the Bronx, had become a sanctuary of God.

I was bawling, and so was Joe. I'm sure he was sorry to God for all the horrible sins he had committed. As I prayed, an overwhelming sense of compassion poured through me to him. It must have been horrible to be a pimp.

Pimps such as Joe lose their women, and then they have to go out and steal to support their own drug habit. That's why they get the girls. The girls prostitute to support their habits.

I'm not justifying what pimps do, but Joe needed the help of Christ to rescue him.

When I finally got through with my prayer, Joe spun around on his bar stool and reached out both hands to me.

I reached down and we threw our arms around each other. I said under my breath, "God, you're something else!"

Joe and I talked a bit more. I hugged and thanked

him for forgiving me, and a big smile came across his face. He grabbed me and said, "You're okay."

I gave Joe another hug and walked to the door, and I felt I was walking on the proverbial clouds. It felt so good!

Some of my staff were up the street. I told them what had happened, and we all rejoiced together.

The following week I went back to the Bronx again. I was so anxious to witness. I was free, really free!

I pulled our van up on Westchester Street. Not only did I want to tell more girls about Christ, but I was hoping I would run into Joe. I parked the van, slid out of the front seat, and walked around the front of the van to the sidewalk.

Standing right there was Joe.

He quickly pointed his finger at me. "Reverend, stay here. I'll be right back."

He abruptly turned and walked away.

My first thought was, "Joe is going to get his gun and come back to kill me."

I knew a lot of guys who killed people didn't carry their gun on them. If they got arrested with a gun, they would spend a long time in jail. So what they would usually do was hide the gun. Then they'd get it out, use it, and put it back in its hiding place.

Would Joe do that?

I nervously paced back and forth. Then I got to thinking. Three weeks ago, when I saw Joe in that bar, he was high. Maybe he had forgotten about my apology.

Maybe I should get out of here now. What Joe was doing didn't seem to make any sense.

What was he doing, anyway?

I soon had the answer. As I stared down the street, here came Joe pushing through the crowd. But I still couldn't make out what he was doing.

Then he got closer. Much to my astonishment, Joe had a girl on each arm.

Thank God, it didn't look like he was coming to kill me.

Joe walked right up to me and smiled. "Reverend, tell these girls about Jesus. They need to know the Lord."

Both of these girls were prostitutes, and I had the wonderful privilege of sharing the gospel with them.

I ran into Joe a few more times on the streets. He had become my friend, and it was always great to see him. Without the fear of getting murdered.

I wish I could tell you Joe lived happily ever after. But he didn't. A couple months later he got into an argument and killed a guy. A week later someone else killed him.

When I heard about Joe's murder it was tough. But it did teach me a great lesson. God is faithful. If you do what the Lord says, he will bring you through every time.

And I have a great report about Becky.

She did complete our program and went on to Bible College. Today she is an outstanding Christian who has a wonderful husband. On occasion she'll come by to our Home in California and speak to our ladies.

She's a great preacher, and continues to minister to many people.

Is it worth it to risk your life for a Becky? You can be sure it is. And for so many others.

What are those girls who are prostitutes really like?

People respond in various ways to that question. Some think we should lock them up and throw away the key. They deserve jail!

I can understand that, but through the many years Elsie and I have been at the Home, we've come to know these ladies. We've found out that they are some mother's daughter or a father's daughter or someone's sister. They are real human beings.

CHAPTER 2
FINDING OUR FIRST PROSTITUTE

I just wish I could tell you that something dramatic happened to Elsie and me that compelled us to work in a ministry of prostitution and drug addiction.

But unfortunately there is nothing really outstanding other than Elsie and I have felt compelled to help those who are in great need.

It first started when I was pastoring and we began working with delinquent teenagers. Those little girls whose lives were terribly crushed by life's circumstances were in great need of help. We responded and through the years we took a number of them into our home. Many of those girls today are outstanding Christians who have married and have families of their own.

When we came to work with Dave Wilkerson at Teen Challenge and heard about these ladies, that same spirit of love and compassion reached out to them. As we came to love and understand, we discovered they were in even worse circumstances than those teenage girls we had helped.

Even though we had a burden to help these ladies

who had fallen so far we really, at the beginning, had never met a prostitute.

And how do you find a prostitute on a busy street in Brooklyn?

It was in 1967 that Elsie and I had talked to one of the fellows at the Brooklyn Teen Challenge Center. He said if we were looking for prostitutes, we should go to Fourth and Atlantic.

Anxiously, we headed in that direction.

As Elsie and I stood on Fourth and Atlantic in Brooklyn, for the life of us we couldn't figure out who was a prostitute. We had never met one before.

When I was a young boy, my father, who was a great Christian, had warned me about prostitutes. He said, "John, prostitutes are filthy — they need a bath. They are ugly, they have no teeth, and furthermore they're full of diseases." I never forgot that.

As Elsie and I watched various ladies walk by that evening, we didn't know if they were prostitutes or not.

I kept looking for the caricature my father had described . . . toothless, ugly, full of disease. But there didn't seem to be that type of woman on the street that evening.

Elsie and I both come from sheltered backgrounds, and we had never been around a person who had been a prostitute and drug addict.

24

Now what?

The guy who had told us where to come had also warned us that it was a dangerous area. As we stood there, a cop approached us and abruptly asked, "What are you doing here?"

His question got me. I just couldn't blurt out that I was looking for a prostitute. I had to think of something quick! "Oh, we're out here to tell people about Jesus," I said smiling.

The cop glared at me, "Sir, you can get killed on this corner trying to give that message."

I still couldn't bring myself to explain the whole reason we were there. I just knew the cop wouldn't understand.

But I did tell him we were from a ministry that helps drug addicts. He didn't seem convinced.

As he started to walk away, he commanded us, "Be careful."

I watched him walk across the street and stop. He turned to stare at us.

We kept looking for that girl. And I kept glancing over at the cop. He had his arms folded, glaring our way.

I know now what he was thinking. He wasn't going to let a couple of innocent looking tourist types get killed on his beat!

Then a guy walked by looking like he needed help I stopped and introduced myself, then began to witness to the guy. I found out he was a drug addict, so I told him how he could be saved and that Teen Challenge was a good place for him to go.

He seemed like a nice guy. We eventually ended our conversation and he walked away.

Still no prostitute.

Elsie and I finally gave up. We went back to the Center rather discouraged.

A few days later we decided to go back to that same area.

This time when we got there, there was no cop. We were going to be on our own.

Again we went through the same process. I saw a girl walking toward me. I was nervous and didn't know if I could approach her. Finally, at the last moment, I held my breath as she walked by.

This just wouldn't do. Somehow we had to find out where those girls were! I said a short prayer under my breath, "Lord, please direct us to a girl who needs you."

No sooner had I breathed that prayer than I saw walking toward us the guy we had spoken to a few weeks ago. He was "that drug addict." And I remembered his name — George.

George recognized us and smiled. I thought I

might as well get this over with. "George, my wife and I are looking for a prostitute to tell about Jesus. Are there any of that type of girl around here?"

No sooner had I gotten the words out of my mouth than George turned and yelled down the street, "Hey Heidi, come here!"

The girl he had yelled at started walking toward us. As I looked at her I wondered if this was going to be the prostitute we were looking for. It couldn't be. Heidi was beautiful. She had long black hair, and as she got closer, a very warm smile. She wasn't ugly. She wasn't filthy. She even had teeth! I didn't know if she was full of disease or not, but this didn't fit the description of the girl my dad had talked about.

Heidi walked up to us. George said, "Heidi, I want to have you meet some good people."

"Heidi is what you are looking for," George said. "She's a prostitute working out here to support a drug habit."

I was shocked. I thought Heidi would be shocked too, with the blunt words George was using. She just smiled at us.

Elsie and I had the wonderful opportunity of telling Heidi about Jesus, that He could set her free from her drug addiction and the ways of the street.

We invited Heidi to come to our home. She didn't come then. But later on a miracle happened.

Heidi did come to us for help. And today she and her husband are missionaries in the Caribbean, along with their two children.

She keeps in contact with us, and I believe it is very significant that the first girl we talked to on the street is a wonderful Christian today.

To this very day, one of the great thrills and challenges of this ministry is our evangelism on the street.

CHAPTER 3
THE VIOLENT STREETS
OF EVANGELISM

Elsie and I have a long list of things we do at the Walter Hoving Home.

My day usually starts at 5:15 spending 45 minutes in Bible study. After that I usually spend an hour in prayer seeking God's guidance for the responsibility of the day.

We eat with the ladies and after breakfast have another time of prayer with them. Then it is to the office for answering mail, planning fund raising activities, telephone calls, staff development, program development, and writing. In addition, I serve on the board at the Walter Hoving Home, The Advisory Board of the Salvation Army, serve on the Los Angeles County Commission on Prostitution, serve as chairman of the board of The Christian Chaplain Services, and am a Rotary Club member.

Elsie's activities as Program Administrator in California are involved in counseling, scheduling, visiting jails, conducting interviews and giving people lots of hugs.

However, of all the things Elsie and I must do at the Walter Hoving Home, we enjoy evangelism on the streets and jails the most.

But it can get dangerous.

Like the time we were recently on Sunset Boulevard. We had taken a van load of friends to go out on the streets witnessing.

As I drove down Hollywood Boulevard, I saw a cop car pulled alongside the curb. The young lady who looked like a prostitute was leaning into a cop car.

I slowed down. I knew in just a moment the cop would reach out and handcuff the girl, and she would be sent to jail.

But all of a sudden, the cop pulled away and left the girl standing there. I couldn't believe it.

The police in Los Angeles are very adept at picking girls off the street. The only problem is, as soon as they get out of jail, they're back on the street again. We have found our effective ministry is ministering to the ladies while they are in jail. After that contact they don't have to go back out to the street. They then come directly to us.

Since the girl was just standing alone, we stopped.

Here's the tactic Elsie and I use . . . I usually stop the van or car and Elsie gets out and makes the first contact with the girl.

The girls on the street tell me that I look like a narcotics police officer. Whenever they see me they want to run. But Elsie, who is affectionately known as Mom B, has a winning smile. She stops everybody in their tracks!

I pulled the van past the girl a little bit and Elsie got out with one of our visitors. A few moments later, I saw Elsie leading the girl back to the van.

Elsie introduced her to me. The girl knew about us because she had read my books in jail and wanted to meet me.

Then we began to witness to her about Jesus.

She told us her story. Just a few minutes before we arrived, her pimp had beaten her up and she wanted to escape.

She saw a cop car coming down Sunset Boulevard and stopped it. As soon as the cops pulled over to the curb she said, "Arrest me right now. I want to get away from my pimp."

The cop said, "We can't arrest you for something like that." Then she said to the cop, "Okay, see that guy walking down the street? As soon as he gets next to me I'm gonna proposition him. You listen to what I say, then you jump out and arrest me for prostitution, okay?"

The girl turned to me and said, "Just as I got through asking the cop to arrest me, they pulled away."

And that's when we pulled up.

"Where's your pimp?" I asked her.

She pointed toward the corner and said, "He's down there. And he's got a loaded gun."

I certainly didn't want the guy blasting away at me with all these visitors in the van. And yet I wanted to reach out to her and help her.

Elsie said to the girl, "Why don't you just hop in?"

I stiffened. I knew what would happen if she just jumped in. Undoubtedly her pimp would start firing at us.

The girl said, "I can't do that. My pimp would probably kill me."

I certainly did agree with her on that. There are violent and vicious "Joe Locos" all over America.

Elsie and I talked a little bit more. Then Elsie said again, "Just jump in."

Before I knew what was happening, the girl leaped into the van.

I wanted to yell at her to get out for fear of the bullets. But I had only one thing to do — try to make it without getting killed.

Fortunately the van was running while we were talking. I slammed the throttle to the floor and we lunged forward.

The corner was just a few feet away and I quickly

turned right, with tires squealing and the smell of burnt rubber in the air.

I ducked and held my breath. We got around the corner safely and then up the street.

I kept listening for those shots, hunched down over the wheel and driving furiously to get out of there.

We took another turn, and then another. I glanced at the girl. Both of us were smiling.

We came back home and were able to provide a safe place for this young lady.

She gave her heart to Christ and stayed a few days. Then she decided to get out of the area and go back home.

Thank God we had the opportunity to rescue her, though it could have cost us our lives.

I just wish you could go out on the street with us to talk with the young women who are prostitutes and drug addicts. If you approach them the right way, these young ladies really will listen to what you have to say.

And there are many ways in which you can present the gospel.

One summer a group from a Christian College came to spend time with us to participate in evangelism outreaches.

They played music, and we'd take a couple of

former addicts to give their testimonies at a street meeting.

One particular night we were up in the same area where Joe Loco hung out. The later the hour, the more addicts there will be. This particular time, it was around midnight when we were out on the street playing music. As a couple of former addicts gave their testimonies, the crowd kept getting bigger. I started preaching and it continued to grow.

Then we had a problem. The crowd was so big it was spilling over into the street.

A cop car came up and I had to stop preaching. The cops thought it was a riot, and they jumped out and headed toward me.

I explained to one officer what we were doing, and he seemed relieved that it wasn't a riot.

In fact, he stood out in the street directing traffic around the large crowd.

After I spoke I invited people to receive Christ right there on the street.

As I bowed my head to pray for the people who had responded, all of a sudden I heard people crying.

In fact, it got so intense that I opened my eyes because I thought something else was happening.

To this day, I have never felt such a presence of the Holy Spirit as I did that night up there in the Bronx. It seemed as though the Lord himself was there with legions of angels.

Many people received Christ that night. Years after that happened, people came to our Home and to other programs who had first encountered Christ there.

A street meeting is not the only way. On December 24, 1990, Christmas Eve, I had an idea for Christmas afternoon.

Here at the Home we celebrate Christmas on Christmas Eve. Then on Christmas Day we have the traditional dinner and our ladies have their families come visit them.

In the afternoon, after Christmas dinner, there is kind of a low for me.

We had received a huge supply of candy canes, so that afternoon I took Sue and Jessica, two of our girls in the program, out on the street with me.

You must understand that drug addicts never have a holiday. When you are addicted to drugs you've got to shoot drugs every day. That means seven-days-a-week, fifty-two weeks a year. No days off. No holidays. I knew that even on Christmas Day, the junkies would be on the streets.

Sue, Jessica and I took the candy canes and our tracts to the street.

You should've been with us that day!

Never before had we had such a great reception. I

must confess I don't know whether it was the candy canes or the fact that those girls had no other friends on the street except us that Christmas Day.

We passed out all our candy canes and tracts. I wish we had had more.

I decided to go to the store and try to get more candy canes. Yes, there was a grocery store open.

We bought more candy canes and I stood in line to pay for them. Ahead of me was a group of people who looked very poor. It looked like a mother, a daughter who was expecting, and another little girl.

I noticed they were buying a single package of chicken. They counted their money carefully as I watched.

The older woman counted her money out to the penny to pay for the package of chicken.

As I stood there my heart went out to them. God had given me so much, but these dear people would have so little this Christmas.

The Lord spoke to me about a $50 bill I had in my wallet. I don't often carry around $50 bills, but I just happened to have one left over from a vacation we had taken.

The Holy Spirit told me to give that money to that poor woman.

I looked for the opportunity after I paid for the

candy. The little group walked across the parking lot. They didn't even get into a car. I knew they were that poor. Sue, Jessica, and I watched them walking along the street.

I pulled out of the parking lot and down the street.

As I pulled alongside them, Sue was sitting on the passenger's side. I said, "Sue, give this to the ladies right there."

Sue looked at the money, then back at me. She began to cry. I began to cry, too.

Sue slipped out of the car and handed the money to the lady. The lady looked at the money, then stared at Sue. I am sure this poor woman had no idea what in the world was happening.

But I did. The Lord wanted to bless those people through me. As we drove off, somehow I felt that they were Christians and God had answered their prayers for a special Christmas dinner.

We went back to the streets, gave out the candy we had bought and returned home.

As Elsie and I went back to the jails to minister, every so often we'd run into someone who had gotten a candy cane that Christmas Day.

It was a highlight of their day and even opened the doors to minister to those who received the candy.

Witnessing on the streets does require learning the technique.

I am not talking about a technique you might learn through some special seminar. I have heard all kinds of things about how you should witness on the streets.

Some sincere people think you should dress like those on the street. You know, beads around the neck, the shirt unbuttoned to the belly button and so forth. Not really.

In fact, sometimes I am out there witnessing in my pinstriped suit if it is convenient. I belong to the Rotary Club in downtown Los Angeles, and after the Rotary meeting sometimes I will swing by an area where the girls are hanging out and witness in my suit.

The most important thing is not how you dress, but whether or not you really care about the people on the street.

However, you must become street wise.

Let me try to explain.

When witnessing to prostitutes you never want to interfere with them if they are about to make connections with a trick. (A "trick" or "john" is the guy they are propositioning.)

The tricks and johns are sometimes nervous when trying to connect with a girl. And, furthermore, the girls really resent it when you interfere with their transactions.

The other problem is the pimps. You've got to be careful, and I'll tell you honestly, you can get shot.

The streets of some of our cities are very violent. The pimps place no value on your life.

When we are on the street and I'm talking to a girl, I try to find out where the pimp is located. Usually, if I look across the street, he will be leaning on a light pole or against a building.

If he is close by and walks toward me, I immediately stop talking to the girl and walk toward the pimp and introduce myself to him.

I found this out from experience. If you can separate yourself from the girl, when you begin to talk to the pimp, be sincerely concerned about him. Ask questions like, "It's really tough here on the street, isn't it?"

Get to know those pimps and, if you can receive this, even become their friend. They have no other friends. Their life is dangerous and they can easily get killed by other pimps or be sent away to prison by the police.

I know some people think all pimps ought to be shot. It's hard to believe that Jesus also died for them.

One time when I was witnessing on the street, I saw a pimp walking toward me. I immediately left the girl I was talking with and started talking with him. But I didn't spend enough time with him. I cut our conversation short, got in the car and drove off.

After I drove around the block, I saw him with the girl I had talked to. He was beating her knuckles with a beer bottle because she had reached out for one of our tracts.

Next time I was more careful. I spent more time with the pimps to save the girls from getting beaten.

It was in that same area, a short time later, that I encountered another violent pimp.

I was coming from a Rotary Club meeting and had decided to do some witnessing on the way back to the Home.

I went to an area where I knew the girls were hanging out and drove down the street by myself. I usually don't like to go by myself because it can get dangerous, but sometimes I do take the chance.

As I got into the area, I saw a girl standing on the corner. I couldn't quickly pull over to the curb to reach her so I had to go around the block.

My first glance told me she was shapely and quite attractive. She was undoubtedly getting a lot of customers. I drove around the block and pulled up to her. Then I rolled down the window and motioned her to come over. I gave her the usual approach as I extended a tract toward her, "Here's something for you to read."

She looked at me.

"I'm John Benton from the Walter Hoving Home. Ever hear of us?" Then I smiled at her.

She smiled back. "Yeah, I know who you are. I read your books in jail."

She came up to the window. I looked at her face. This young lady looked rather attractive from a distance, but close up, I noticed her face was deeply scarred.

When she spoke to me, I saw that half her teeth were missing. Her skin was ashen and her eyes were sunk back in her head. I began to tell her about what the Lord could do. She just stood there staring at me.

I even offered to take her off the street and bring her home right then. She said, "I sleep in the alley next to a dumpster down there." She pointed down the street. It looked dangerous.

Then she said, "Besides that, I'm full of syphilis."

As I looked at her, I felt a great pity. This was somebody's daughter who desperately needed help. She had been born into this world, and how she got into this horrible life I don't know.

You could see the hurt in her eyes. I said again, "Hop in, I'll bring you to a place of love and safety."

Much to my surprise she began to back up. She said, "I'm sorry, I'm sorry, it won't work for me, it just won't work for me."

I raised my voice a little. "Yes it will! It has worked for thousands, and it can work for you."

She continued to back up. "There's no hope for me."

She turned and walked down the street. My first impulse was to jump out of the car and chase her. I'd grab her and put her in my car and bring her home even if it took force. But I knew better than that. Who knew what would happen if she started screaming? It would be senseless to try something like that.

I rolled up the window. I was so disappointed.

As I drove away I kept thinking about that girl. I didn't look on her as a prostitute. Or a junkie. I saw her as somebody's daughter who needed help. And she even could have been my own daughter.

I remember one time I was watching the World Vision documentary on the starving children of Africa.

As those scenes flashed across that television screen I looked into the pathetic eyes of those little children with bloated stomachs and frail arms and legs.

The sight, as you've probably seen, is hard to take. But as I kept staring at the screen one little boy looked like my grandson.

As I stared at that little guy I thought what my response would be if it really was my grandson. I was overcome by emotion and began to weep. That boy I was looking at was somebody's grandson.

To say the least, I wrote out a good-sized check to World Vision . . . to help somebody's grandson.

And that's the way Elsie and I feel about every

lady. Each one is somebody's daughter. Could be yours. Could be mine. But somebody has to love them and take them in from the hell of this world.

And that's why we're here. Both of our homes are filled with somebody's daughters. Yes, they are addicts. They are prostitutes. They're doing terrible things. But they are somebody's daughters.

We continue to go out on the streets. Though I was rejected by that lady who said there was no hope, others have accepted our invitation to come to our Home.

Thank God for all the ladies who are here now.

CHAPTER 4
COPS CALL IT THE WORST
PLACE IN TOWN

It was one of those late night calls.

In our ministry, whenever the phone rings after midnight it's not someone calling just to say hello. These calls are always emergencies; many times they are life-threatening ones.

And this was no exception.

The girl identified herself — Valerie.

Elsie and I knew Valerie from the streets. Try as we may to win her over to the Lord, we just could not get her free from her pimp. And of all the names to have for a pimp, his name was Bittersweet.

Valerie had been a drug addict and prostitute for many years. She hung out in the worst part of the city, Main Street. No, not Main Street of some small town, but Main Street of Los Angeles. It's in the barrio, and very dangerous.

In fact, a number of years ago I went out under-cover with the Vice Squad of the Los Angeles Police Department. We dressed as a couple old bums and the Vice Sergeant went around in a beat-up old Volkswagen Bug. The thing was really a wreck. It didn't even have seatbelts.

As we were taking a tour of the city we went by Third and Main. The Sergeant said, "Rev, whatever you do, never get out on the street here. We have twelve muggings a day."

I took note of that.

When Valerie called she wanted me to come rescue her. Bittersweet had beaten her up again and he was going to kill her.

I asked her where she was. She said, "Third and Main."

A surge of fear went through me. I remembered the words of the Vice Sergeant. "Third and Main."

I wanted to stall. And yet, by the desperation in her voice, I knew I had to do something right now.

At that time we had two interns from a Bible College in the Midwest working with us. I decided to take them with me. I was sure these two little blondes from Iowa would never forget the experience.

And yet I was somewhat hesitant. I knew about Bittersweet. He could kill, and I hesitated about taking the two girls into that dangerous environment.

Elsie was trying to get some sleep after a very long day, so I didn't think I should have her get dressed and go with me. I finally decided to take the two girls.

I went across the street to meet the two interns and we all got into my car.

We drove down to Main street and immediately headed toward Third.

I had been by there a few times before. You can't describe the evil that is there. Those are demon-infested streets where all types of crime and perversion take place.

We looked for Valerie. I didn't spot her so we circled around and went down Main Street again. No Valerie.

Then the thought hit me. I was probably too late. Valerie might be dead by now.

We kept searching and searching. No Valerie.

As time wore on, I was tempted to get out of the car and ask somebody. But I knew better. I would either be killed or mugged for sure.

This reminded me of the time in New York when I was doing some witnessing on 110th and Madison Avenue. I saw this guy with a chain in his hand. It looked like he had been walking his dog, but the dog had run away.

I must admit, in those days, I wasn't as street-wise as I am now. I would never do now what I did then — get out of my car and walk the street in such a dangerous area.

But God was with me. The guy with the chain immediately responded to the gospel. I found out he was a drug addict. Then I asked him about his dog. He laughed. "I don't have a dog."

I pointed at the chain. "Then what's that for?"

He smiled. "It's like this, I see a guy walking down the street, come up behind him and whip the chain around his neck. As soon as he reaches up to try to stop that chain around his neck, I put my knife in his ribs. It works every time."

I drew back. He was looking at me. I knew if he was going to rob me, he wasn't going to get much. But I didn't want him trying it.

"Won't the people in the street hear this guy crying for help and come to his rescue?" I asked.

He laughed again. "Look up and down this street. All those people are drug addicts. They would only laugh at the guy."

Now here I was on Main Street in Los Angeles. I knew better than to get out of the car.

I decided to take another trip along Main Street. Somehow I felt that Valerie was near here. We just had to find her.

Slowly we kept cruising Main Street. We looked at the people and many of them glared back at us. I'm sure they were wondering what this white guy was doing with these two blondes. Certainly, we were out of character for that area.

As I crossed Fourth, and was heading toward Third, I was looking to my right. There was a greasy chicken fast food place, and as I glanced in, there sat

Valerie.

I saw her pimp. I had never met him before, but being on the streets it doesn't take long to recognize pimps.

Backing up, I pulled over to the curb where Bittersweet couldn't see me.

And then I waited.

As soon as Valerie came out that door I'd grab her and we would take off. I would take my chances.

As I sat there with these two Iowa blondes, people came up and would stare in the window and make remarks. To say the least, I was scared to death. And I knew how the two girls felt.

I kept waiting, but still no Valerie.

A guy walked over to my window. We had the door locked, so I lowered the window about an inch.

He said, "Man, what are you doing here?"

I didn't know whether I should really let him know. What was this guy up to, anyway? I knew it wasn't anything good by the tone of his voice.

But then I thought, well, I'd just tell him what I'm doing.

I introduced myself and told him about the Walter Hoving Home. "That girl in there needs help. I'm trying to get her out here."

He said, "Hey, I'd be happy to walk in there with you. But I want to tell you something, it's dangerous on these streets."

The guy didn't have to tell me that. The Vice Sergeant had warned me.

Then he said, "When you step out of the car, be sure and take your wallet out and leave it on the seat. That's the first thing they'll go for."

Whenever I'm in a dangerous situation I try to stay in touch with the Lord. I keep asking Him for His wisdom and guidance. I don't want to do anything foolish. At that moment I asked the Lord a direct question. "Can I trust this guy?"

And that still, small voice whispered to me. Thank God, He'll speak to your heart if you're tuned in. The Holy Spirit said, "He wants you to open your locked door because, as soon as you put your wallet on the seat, he plans to grab it and run."

Under my breath I thanked the Lord. Then I looked at the guy. I wasn't through with him yet.

"I can't get out of the car for fear of getting robbed," I said, "but I'll tell you what I will do. I'll give you two dollars if you go in there and get that girl out for me."

The guy smiled. "Man, I just got out of prison today. Two dollars looks like a big deal!"

And then I wondered if I wasn't going to be set up.

I'd give him the two dollars and he'd take off.

I said, "Can you be trusted?" I asked.

He smiled again. "Yeah, you can sure trust me."

It was worth two dollars to take a chance. I just had to get Valerie.

I took out my wallet and pulled out two ones. I pushed them through the open slot of the window.

The guy snatched the money, spun around and walked toward the front of my car. My eyes were glued on him. Would he take off? Much to my surprise, he crossed the sidewalk and went into the chicken place.

I couldn't see all the way in because I had backed up the car, but I didn't dare let Bittersweet see me there.

We waited. Nothing happened.

Maybe the poor guy was hungry since he just got out of prison that day. Maybe he was buying a couple pieces of chicken.

We waited some more.

And then it happened. An old guy right next to our car had been jumped. Two guys pinned him down and were mugging him.

The guy screamed out for help.

I wanted to bolt out of that door and come to his

rescue. But I just couldn't. I knew what would happen to me — they would mug me too.

Have you ever been in a situation where you are really torn between two conflicting impulses? As a Christian, should I take my chances and try to help that guy. Or would that be foolishness, not using the common sense God has given me.

I looked at the poor guy. They had his wallet and he was still yelling. He kept hollering, "Police! Police! Police!"

But nobody on the street responded. The two guys got his wallet and ran down the street.

The poor old guy slowly struggled to his feet and wandered off in the opposite direction.

I felt so confused and frustrated. I wanted to help and yet I didn't dare. Still I waited for the guy to come out with Valerie.

Then I thought, that guy probably knew Bittersweet and they were in there laughing. They had ripped me off for two bucks.

But I waited a little bit more.

Finally the guy came out. Without Valerie.

He walked over to the car. I rolled down the window just slightly.

He said, "The guy in there wants to talk to you. Come on in and talk to him."

The Holy Spirit spoke again, "It's a set-up."

"I don't feel right about getting out of the car," I told him.

"Well, the guy in there wants to talk to you," he insisted. "There's no way that girl's going to come out here. You've got to go talk to the guy first."

I was really frustrated. And yet, as I looked back on that night God had other purposes in mind.

At that time, I had to say, "There's no way I'm going to get out of the car."

"Then there is no way that girl is coming out here," he repeated.

I didn't know what was going to happen next. I didn't want anybody pulling a gun on me and I knew I had to get out of there right then.

"Thanks for your help anyway," I sighed.

We left Main Street and returned to the Home. I still had horribly mixed emotions. Should I have pressed this and tried to rescue Valerie? Or had I done the right thing? Was it really God speaking?

I crawled back in bed, but I couldn't sleep. Had I really missed it?

Again I prayed and asked the Lord to keep Valerie safe.

This story has a beautiful ending. Later on, Valerie got arrested. She did survive the many times Bittersweet beat her up.

And because of going to jail and meeting us again, she came to the Home for help. Today, Valerie is a tremendous Christian who really knows the Lord. She has graduated from our program and God has blessed her by reuniting her with her son.

While Valerie was in the program, we talked about the incident with Bittersweet. And then I found out why God didn't let us rescue Valerie that night. "I knew you were out there," Valerie told me. "But I also knew if I tried anything, you would be in great danger. So I thought the best thing to do was to sit there and do nothing."

Then I knew the Lord had everything under control. If Valerie had tried to get into the car, Bittersweet might have shot both of us. For that matter, maybe all four of us. Those pimps put very little value on human life.

How I thank God for the wisdom of Valerie! I thank God for his voice and protection.

CHAPTER 5
SO, YOU WANT TO
WRITE A BOOK

God has opened an enormous door for our ministry through the books I've written.

Sometimes people have asked me how I got into book writing.

It really started with my friend David Wilkerson.

Many years ago Dave and I were traveling down the New Jersey Turnpike, coming back from a meeting late at night. Dave turned to me and said, "John, why don't you write a book about the ministry you and Elsie have with the ladies."

I laughed and said, "Dave, I hate English."

I thought writing a book had to do with English. It does, but I found out later there are many different approaches to writing.

Dave said, "Well, just put something down on paper. We can have someone help you out with the writing of it."

"Is that all you have to do?" I asked.

"Yes," Dave said. "My friends at Revell Publishers might be interested in it, and they can help you with the project."

Dave made arrangements for me to meet with Bill Barbour, the president of Revell.

And I started my first book, DEBS, DOLLS AND DOPE.

I usually wrote between one and three in the morning. I wrote only one draft out in long hand on yellow legal pads and found that writing early in the morning was just right for me. We usually got in from the street about that time and I couldn't sleep, so I'd reach for my legal pad.

And that started it all.

Since that time I have written 39 books. This is my 40th.

The Holy Spirit has really used the books in our jail and street ministry.

We've given them away by the thousands to the ladies in jail. They read the books and through them they have come to know us. We stamp an imprint in the front of the book telling if they need help to call us collect. And many of them do.

My first book about the girls is called CARMEN. It has now been translated into a number of languages and continues to have a ministry here in the States and in Canada.

When I was writing CARMEN, I had an experience I shall never forget.

One night I went up to the Bronx to minister.

That's the place I mentioned before, where Joe Loco had come from.

There, on the corner of Fox and Westchester, stood a girl by the name of Patti.

I walked up to her and introduced myself, "I'm John Benton from the Walter Hoving Home. We have a home for ladies who are addicts and prostitutes."

She stepped back and looked at me rather suspiciously. I had the feeling she didn't believe me.

Then I began to witness to her about Christ.

I told Patti she didn't have to live this way any longer. I gave her a tract about our ministry and as I handed it to her she said, "Oh my God, I thought you were a trick."

We both laughed. The ladies in the street usually get me mixed up with a cop from the Vice Squad, but Patti thought I was a trick. I really don't know what either of those types of people say to prostitutes, but there probably aren't too many cops or tricks who witness to them about Christ.

Then Patti said, "My old man is standing in a darkened doorway down the street, and he's signaling for me to bring you down there."

I glanced down Fox Street. It was dark and looked very dangerous.

57

She continued. "He has a lead pipe in his hand. When you walk by him, he hits you over the head and knocks you out. Then we'll take your wallet, your watch, and rings . . . whatever you've got."

So that was the ploy Patti normally used. It is quite common in some areas of the inner city.

I started to get scared. Patti must have noticed. She said, "I better run down there and tell him who you are."

I certainly didn't want him coming after me, so I said, "Yeah, that's a good idea. Run down and tell him who I am."

Patti turned and quickly went down the darkened street. I stood there, waiting. It was too dark to see where she had gone. My first impulse was to walk into that darkness and get Patti again. She had really seemed to respond to what I was saying. But then, would that be the wise thing to do?

I waited. But no Patti. I was having this terrible inner turmoil. Should I try to get her? Or would her old man be so desperate for drugs that he could care less who I was. I had heard stories of people getting killed like this.

Finally I decided not to risk it. I walked back up Westchester where the other staff were.

We did some more witnessing and went home.

I think it was about two weeks later when who

should call us wanting help. You guessed it! It was Patti.

We picked up Patti and brought her to the Home. Then we put her into the "kicking room." She had a long run, and I knew she was going to kick real bad cold turkey. This is an instantaneous withdrawal from drugs.

Kicking cold turkey is an experience you'll never forget.

Patty was so appreciative to us for helping her out. Her first day wasn't too bad. But the second day was the worst.

Elsie and I had our bedroom next to the kicking room. Before I retired for the night I dropped in to see how Patti was doing. Patti was not looking good. She was terribly sick. The poor ladies have terribly high fevers, hot and cold flashes and diarrhea. I've seen hundreds kick, and everytime it wrenches my heart to see these poor girls suffer.

I tried to give Patti some words of encouragement. I also shared with her the need to trust God during this tough time.

I went to bed. Knowing Patti was next door, I couldn't fall asleep right away. But eventually I did.

It must have been about two o'clock in the morning when I heard a blood-curdling scream. "Jesus! Jesus!"

I quickly jumped out of bed. I didn't know if the

rapture had taken place or what, so I looked for Elsie. She was still lying in bed. She's very spiritual, so I knew the rapture had not come yet.

I slipped on my bathrobe and went down the hall into the kicking room. There I saw Patti with another one of our ladies in the program.

"Lisa, what happened?" I asked.

Lisa said, "Patti was in such pain that I was praying for her, and I told her to cry out to Jesus."

One of the things that always blesses me in this ministry is the love and concern each of our ladies has for the new girls during the awful time of kicking cold turkey. They will rub one another's aching backs . . . help them into a hot tub . . . do anything they can because they've been through it, too.

But I knew what had happened in this particular circumstance. Somehow Patti had gotten her theology mixed up. She thought the degree of help depended upon the volume, so she wanted to make sure Jesus really heard her!

Then I asked Patti, "Would you like for me to pray for you?"

I looked at her ashen face, those eyes that pleaded for help. She answered, "Please."

I reached out and put my hand on her shoulder.

I do believe in the healing power of Christ. It obviously doesn't happen every time I pray, but I still believe Jesus has come to heal us.

And thank God, we've seen some miraculous healings take place. I've seen some of our ladies instantaneously delivered from kicking cold turkey. Many others still have to go through the ordeal. But still I pray and believe the best I can that Jesus will heal them.

As I came to the close of my prayer, I have to tell you exactly what happened.

Just as I lifted my hand from Patti's shoulder she rolled over towards me. Then she emptied her stomach all over my bare feet! Because of Patti's physical ordeal, that which splattered over my feet I could not describe to you! It was the worst looking stuff you've ever seen.

But I didn't flinch. I turned and walked out of the room and got a mop out of the bathroom. I washed off my feet then grabbed the mop and headed back to the kicking room.

While Patti lay there watching me, I mopped up the floor, then went and washed out the mop.

I walked out the bathroom and across the hall into Patti's room. I asked Patti if she'd like to have one of the staff stay up with her. She said no, that would be okay. She'd just kick it alone.

I spoke with her a few more moments and then went back to bed.

Elsie had managed to sleep through that whole mess. Sleep did not come easy, but eventually I dozed off.

About six months later I was still writing my book CARMEN. I wanted to record the girls' impressions when they first come to the home. I got about five or six ladies to sit down on the floor and began to ask them about their feelings.

One of the ladies was Patti. After a few girls had shared their feelings Patti raised her hand.

"Yes, Patti," I prompted.

"Do you remember the night I was kicking?"

"I'll never forget that night as long as I live," I answered, and we both laughed.

Then Patti got very serious. She said, "I can't tell you how I've hated men through the years, because of my drug habit. I knew I was a prostitute on the street, and yet I felt I had become a slave to evil men's lust and perversion. I had to do what I had to do to support my habit, but developed a terrific hatred toward men."

I understood what she was saying. A girl who must earn money to get drugs to stop her terrible pain is subjected to all types of indignities and perversions. I cannot tell you of the terrible things these ladies go through. It is absolutely unbelievable.

I also knew about the hatred toward men.

Patti continued, "My hatred toward men was so strong, but I want to tell you what happened to me the night I was kicking."

I leaned forward. Patti hadn't said a whole lot that night. What was she trying to express now?

"That night, when I saw you mopping up my puke, I knew Christ was real," Patti declared.

I looked into Patti's eyes. There were tears. Then it hit me too. I felt a lump in my throat and the tears came down my cheeks. The other girls began to weep as well.

I had no idea in this whole wide world that someone was watching to see if I was a real Christian.

I'm sure if you were in the same circumstances, you would've done the same thing I did. To me, at that time, it didn't seem like a big deal. It was just doing what had to be done.

But I've learned a big lesson . . . it isn't what you say that counts, it's what you do. Mopping Patti's vomit left a lasting impression on her.

Today, people want to experience Christianity, and not just hear about it. The greatest influence we can have as a Christian is not through what we say, but through what we do.

That's how it is today in this ministry. We have to live among the girls, and that can be a "good news, bad news" situation. The good news is that we have the wonderful opportunity to demonstrate what Christ is all about by what we do. The bad news is, of course, that we have pressure on us to live a life committed to the Lord. I must say we don't always succeed. But when we have failed, the Lord has given us His grace to ask for forgiveness.

Patti continued in the program and learned to love Jesus with all her heart. She has taught me one of the greatest lessons I will ever learn.

The Facilities in Pasadena, CA

The Staff and Girls in Pasadena

The Facilities in New York

The Staff and Girls in New York

CHAPTER 6
WANT TO GET MARRIED?

One of the first opportunities for ministry with our books happened with a girl by the name of Denise.

Denise was a hard-core heroin addict from New York City. She found out there was a good dope dealer near Garrison, in a small town called Middletown.

Denise left the city and went up to buy her dope. As she was leaving town, the police pulled her over and caught her for drug possession.

They put her in their little jail and Denise sat there, really bewildered by the whole experience. She had, of course, been in jail before, but never in such a small one.

A Christian woman visited the jail on Sundays to minister to the few ladies who were there. She gave Denise a copy of my book, CARMEN.

Denise read it and made contact with us. After serving her time there, she came into the Home.

Today, Denise is an outstanding Christian. She's married to a wonderful guy. Her little boy, who was in foster care while she was in the Home, is now in college. He, too, is a great Christian.

Denise had an unusual experience, although I've since found out it has happened to a number of our ladies. They will marry someone from a foreign country for an amount of anywhere from $100 to $500.

Denise was still on the street. Once, while she was standing on a street corner in Manhattan, a guy came up to her and started talking to her. "Will you marry me?" he asked.

Denise thought that was rather odd. She wasn't about to marry a stranger!

"For $500," the man went on. Denise was suddenly very interested.

"What do I have to do?" she demanded.

"Just come down and get the marriage license. I want to stay in this country."

Denise found out the guy was from Germany. He liked it here, and wanted to stay in the U.S.

Another one of our ladies, Peg, used to go down to Mexico and bring back a Mexican in the trunk of her car. She was a long-time addict, and that's how she made her money.

Peg did very well at it, too.

Not only would she get money for smuggling in the Mexicans, but the Mexicans often had dope stuffed in their pockets. In addition to all this, when Peg got back to Los Angeles, she would marry the Mexican for more money.

Every trip Peg took brought her thousands of dollars.

Now, Denise was going to marry this guy for $500.

They made arrangements, went down and got their license, and got married.

Denise told me this guy wouldn't go to bed with her. He was afraid that Denise had a venereal disease. And he didn't want to catch it.

She stayed around him for about three days and then took off.

He kept in contact with her now and then, but it certainly was no husband-and-wife relationship.

Then one day, while Denise was with us, he called the Home and wanted to meet with Denise.

Denise and I went down to Manhattan and met him for lunch. Actually, he was a very nice guy. He worked for a foreign embassy. He had since found out that, because he worked for the embassy, he had exempt status and could stay in the country. He didn't need to get married the way he had.

He did find out that what he did was fraudulent, and he wanted to get an annulment. He would pay for all the lawyer's fees if Denise was willing to go along with it.

Of course she was. She, too, was concerned about committing that kind of a crime.

It was all worked out, and Denise got out of that fraudulent marriage.

Denise went on to Bible school. While she was attending a local church, she met a young man. Of all things, he was a cop.

But that didn't stop Denise. They fell in love and got married. Today she and her husband and son are faithfully serving God.

We have distributed my books in prisons for several years now.

The prison ministry eventually led to the privilege of my being a volunteer chaplain at one of America's most notorious prisons, the California Institute for Women, commonly known as CIW. This is a maximum security prison, and it is renowned for its women inmates who were involved in the Manson killings.

For a few months I volunteered as the chaplain there. And that led to many wonderful opportunities for Elsie and me to minister to women who are so bound by Satan.

CHAPTER 7
KILLER MILLER

It was Christmas day.

I was asked by the head chaplain at the California Institute for Women if I could be on duty the afternoon and evening of Christmas. My first thought was, "Christmas Day?"

But after considering the opportunity of being able to spend this special Christian holiday with the inmates at a women's prison, I accepted.

When Elsie and I arrived at the prison that afternoon, instead of inmates celebrating, we found a lot of deep depression and discouragement.

Holidays in prison are not a time for celebration. They mean separation from loved ones. In this case, it meant many mothers were separated from their children. And the tragic consequences of the severed relationships have enormous effect not only on the mothers, but on the children as well.

As part of my responsibility as chaplain, I had to go to the main gate and accompany church groups who were to minister in the services.

Fortunately, this Christmas evening we had a group coming. Thank God for those dear friends who would give of themselves for the ladies.

The time for the service came and I started to make my way across the prison yard, from the chaplains office to the entrance of the prison.

I knew we were going to have quite a group that night for chapel service, and I was looking forward to the service with this church group.

As we were coming back across the yard, one of the officers of the prison yelled to me. "Chaplain, can I see you for a minute?"

The call was coming from the Miller building.

The officer was quite urgent in her appeal. Coming from the Miller building, I knew something had happened. This was the place where they housed all those ladies who had committed murder.

Some of these ladies had committed violent murders. In fact, one of the ladies there had fallen in love with her psychiatrist. When he had rejected her advances, she ended up killing him, his wife and two children. There were a number of the same type of inmates in this dormitory.

The other inmates gave the Miller building a nickname. They called it "Killer Miller."

I told the group I was escorting in, to wait right there. I quickly made my way across the lawn and approached the officer who was standing at the doorway of the building.

When I got to her she said, "Chaplain, is there any possible way for you to have a service in this building this evening?"

"There really isn't," I told her, shaking my head. "I just got this group in, and I'm escorting them to the chapel. There is a service over there."

The inmates in the Miller building were restricted in their activities. One of those restrictions was that they had to be locked down after six o'clock so they couldn't attend the evening chapel service on Christmas day.

I knew about the restriction, and I really couldn't do anything about it.

"I really don't have anyone else on duty this evening," I told the officer.

But she was persistent. "Don't you have anyone else who could possibly help us. These inmates have had nothing this whole Christmas season. No chapel service, no nothing. Isn't there some possible way you could do something?"

She kept pleading. I said, "There is no one else on duty except me. It's just my wife and me. That's all, Elsie and me."

"Well, then, would your wife come?" she asked.

Now let me tell you something. You just have to

meet Elsie, my wife. She is known as Mom B and has a heart bigger than the world. I knew what Elsie's response would be to the challenge of conducting chapel in "Killer Miller."

"Well, let me ask her," I said. " I'll be right back."

I took the group to the chapel and settled them in. Elsie was sitting there. "Would you like to have a chapel service over in the Miller building?" I asked her.

I think before I completed the sentence, Elsie was on her feet marching in that direction.

As a chaplain I had my own set of keys. When we got to the Miller dormitory, I unlocked the door and let Elsie in. The officer said the only place they really had to conduct a chapel service was the laundry room. She pointed down the long hallway.

These buildings have very long hallways. On both sides they have cells which were originally made for one person to a cell. But because of the overcrowded conditions of the prison, they have crammed two ladies into each cell.

Every door in prison is locked. I unlocked the laundry room door and told Elsie this was her chapel.

She smiled. It didn't make any difference to her.

I had to lock her in there with the inmates. She was on her own.

I went down the hallway and unlocked myself to

the yard, then went across to the chapel.

Was it really safe to leave Elsie with those inmates who were all murderers, I wondered. Knowing Elsie, she probably would have loved to be taken hostage. She always said she wanted to spend time in jail.

We had our regular chapel service that Christmas night. I kept thinking about Elsie.

After the service I escorted the church group out, then went back to "Killer Miller."

I went through the secured doors and down to the laundry room.

There was Elsie. She was sitting on the floor with all those ladies. Of course, there were no chairs, so they were all making themselves at home.

It seemed like a mother with her children. All the ladies had big smiles on their faces. I could tell they must have had a great time with their very own Mom B.

As we left the building, I ran into the officer who had asked for the service. She said, "Chaplain, this has been the greatest Christmas ever here in the Miller building. I can't thank you enough for what you've done."

Since that time, Christmas Day has taken on a new meaning for me.

While you and I celebrate Christmas this year, there are still thousand of ladies, locked down, who never experience the wonderful joys of Christmas. That is why God has raised up the Walter Hoving Home.

When people visit the Walter Hoving home in Garrison, they are overwhelmed by its beauty. Coming from the hell of the streets of Brooklyn where we almost got killed, to a beautiful 37-acre country estate, is one of the greatest miracles I have ever experienced.

CHAPTER 8

GETTING OUT OF HELL

In the beginning of this ministry, we picked a horrible place to start a girls' home.

It was in Brooklyn on the edge of Bedford-Stuyvesant.

This old home needed paint. Both inside and out. It had no lawn and it needed re-decorating throughout. Believe me it had seen better days. Besides that, it was in a crime-infested, deteriorating neighborhood.

On the left side was a drug dealer. He kept trying to sell drugs to our girls. On the right was a band of revolutionaries. They were trying to overthrow the government and were very subversive.

One day the FBI came to me and explained more about these neighbors. They asked if I wouldn't work with them and monitor their activities. The FBI didn't pay me or anything like that, but I felt it was my duty as an American to try to assist them.

Our house was on a violent street. In fact, we even saw people trying to kill each other with guns. It was dangerous even trying to get from our car to the Home.

Then there were the break-ins. One guy even stole our downspouts from outside of the house because they were copper.

To top it all off, once one of our new girls was sitting on the front steps. As I watched from the living room window, a guy came walking down the street. The girl got up and walked to the sidewalk. Without a moment's hesitation she propositioned him. The next thing I knew, I saw them walking down the street arm in arm.

That scared me. I didn't want people on the block thinking I was operating a house of prostitution. Or maybe they thought I was a pimp. Rumors ran wild anyway about what we were trying to do there.

We brought girls in from the streets, but because of our location, they just wouldn't stay. I just knew we had to have another place. This situation would not do.

The following evening I came in very late from evangelism on the street. Elsie was already in bed, sound asleep. She had had a very long day, too.

Because of the intensity of the streets I can't fall asleep right away, so I usually try to read a little bit.

I sat on the edge of the bed reading a Christian magazine. There was an article in there on the subject of faith. I was trying to believe God for another place.

In this article the writer gave an illustration of two ministers.

One of the ministers wanted to become a tent evangelist, and he was trying to learn the lesson of faith. He prayed, "O God, I just want a tent. And it can be a tent with holes in it. I believe you now for a used tent. I have faith in you that you will give it to me."

And you know what? God gave him that used tent with leaky holes in it. He was happy as a clam and went on down the road preaching the gospel.

The second minister was a pastor. He was believing God for a huge cathedral with plush carpeting, comfortable pews, air conditioning, and a great sound system. He prayed, "God, I believe you are going to give me this huge cathedral. I have faith in you for it. Amen."

And you know what?

That second minister got his huge cathedral!

Both of these men exercised faith in God.

The last line of that article changed my life. It said, "It takes just as much faith to believe God for a leaky tent as it does for a huge cathedral."

I sat there staring at the page. Then I said to myself, "If that's the case, I'm gonna believe God right now for a mansion in the country."

Mind you, there I was sitting in the middle of hell. We had no money. And I had no wealthy friends.

But no matter what, I was believing God for the

81

mansion in the country.

A couple weeks after I read that article, Elsie and I were invited to a dinner party at Paul and Sonya Dilena's home in Long Island.

David and Gwen Wilkerson were to be there, as well as another couple I had not met, Mr. and Mrs. Walter Hoving.

At the dinner party I sat next to Mr. Hoving.

Trying to make conversation with him, I said, "And what do you do?"

"I'm the chairman of Tiffany's," he told me.

I come from a very poor family. We led a very simple life and we were in no way connected with wealth or wealthy people.

When Mr. Hoving said he was from Tiffany's the only thing I could remember was something about Tiffany lamps.

This guy next to me must be a lamp maker, I figured.

I was going to ask him where his lamp factory was located, but before I could, he said, "And what do you do?"

I then told him about Elsie's and my ministry with girls who were addicts and prostitutes. That seemed to catch his attention.

"What are your plans for the future?" he asked.

The Holy Spirit spoke to me. Remember the article on faith? Are you still believing God for a mansion in the country?

I didn't know whether or not I should tell him what I was believing for. Maybe it would be too presumptuous to tell a person I didn't even know about this so-called mansion in the country. In fact, I hadn't even told Elsie what I was believing God for. Maybe she wouldn't understand. I knew it would be absolutely impossible to go from our horrible situation to a mansion in the country.

But I believed what I believed, so I said, "We are looking for a place outside the city."

Mr. Hoving smiled. "I have a friend that might be able to help you out. Why don't you come see me, and we can talk about it."

I then found out who this Mr. Hoving was. Yes, he was the chairman of Tiffany's. But Tiffany's was more than a lamp maker. This was the famous Tiffany & Company on Fifth Avenue in New York City, world renowned for their diamonds and other beautiful jewelry.

Before leaving that evening, I set up an appointment with Mr. Hoving.

When I walked into Tiffany's for the first time, I was overwhelmed by its elegance.

I went up to the fifth floor and into his spacious office. I was shaking all over. I had never experienced anything like this before in my life.

Mr. Hoving made me feel very comfortable. Then he told me he was associated with the Jones Foundation. At one time Mr. Jones had served on the Board of Directors of Tiffany's. Mr. Hoving then made arrangements for me to go down and talk to Mr. Farrell who ran the Jones Foundation.

I went to see Mr. Farrell. I was more direct this time and told them about our need to purchase a place outside the city. I told him it needed to be a big one. Out of that conversation, the Jones Foundation gave us $15,000.00 towards the purchase of a home in the country.

We had heard about an estate that was for sale up in Garrison, New York. Garrison is directly across the river from West Point.

We did locate that estate but the gardener told us it had been sold to someone else.

I was shattered.

By this time we'd looked everywhere for a home. We looked up near the Cascade Mountains. Then off to Long Island. Parts of New Jersey. Nothing.

The Estates we looked at just didn't seem to accommodate us. Some had lots of bedrooms but a small dining room. Others had large dining rooms but few bedrooms. Or not enough bathrooms. Or not enough space for our School for Christian Growth.

84

I was standing there thinking what we would do now.

"There's another place for sale, though," the gardener continued.

"You know, as you come down the road from the golf course, there's a place that kind of sits up on a hill. A Union uses it for a convalescent home, but they want to sell it. They are moving out tomorrow."

"You mean that place with all the lush grass and the stream running down the side of the property?" I asked.

"Yep, that's the one."

"The one that looks like a million dollars?" I asked again.

"Uh-huh. That's it."

"How much do they want for it?" I asked. "Probably a million dollars?"

"Well, I don't really know. It's a beautiful place. Why don't you drop over there and see?"

Boy, was this news! But how much was it going to cost? That thought troubled me, as Elsie and I drove over to the place.

As we drove through the stone entranceway, I looked to my left and saw the crystal-clear swimming pool. At the end of the pool was a twelve-foot-high waterfall. Further up the tree-lined drive way, I could see various other trees I had never seen before — different kinds of pines and cedars. We drove around a small curve and there, straight up the hill, stood the three-story mansion. What a sight! I followed the driveway around the mansion and parked the car.

"Honey," Elsie said, "this place is fantastic! I believe God wants us to have it."

My faith wasn't that strong, but I rang the doorbell.

"Hello, I heard this place was for sale. My wife and I would like to have a look at it," I said to the man who opened the door.

"Come right in. I'm not the man who runs the place, but I'll be glad to show you around," he answered.

As we stepped into the living room, I felt as though we were at home. The walls were paneled halfway and just to the left, was the big sand-colored fireplace. Rust-colored wall-to-wall carpeting covered the floor and set off the many pieces of comfortable, colorful modern furniture. Farther to my left, I could see the dining room, which held six dining tables with matching chairs.

"Here, follow me," the man said. I must have been standing there with my mouth open. We followed him to the right.

"And in this part we have three bedrooms," he said. That was what I wanted to hear — bedrooms! We were desperate for more bedrooms. The beds were all Simmons beds and all the furniture matched.

As we walked through this place, I could hardly believe my ears. The gentleman kept saying, ". . .and here's another bedroom." Fifteen bedrooms and nine bathrooms! The kitchen had a modern institutional dishwasher, a large two-oven gas stove, a large table in the middle and a two-door refrigerator — all in spotless, stainless steel. Two big, deep-freezers stood side by side. I just couldn't get over how well equipped this place was. I could see rows of neatly stacked dishes, and I wondered if they planned to leave any of the furniture or dishes.

Our guide answered my questions before I had a chance to ask.

"And this place is fully furnished," he said. "Everything you see goes with it. Furniture, beds, blankets, sheets, dishes, towels, washcloths, lamps, silverware — everything stays right here."

After going all around the place, including the basement and the third floor, we walked outside and down the hill in the opposite direction from which we had come. Near the bottom of the hill on the right hand side was a long, low, brown and white stucco building that was used as a lodge. When I walked inside, I knew this was just what we needed — a spot to take teen-age girls camping during the hot summer. Girls from the ghettos would really be excited to have a place like this. The guide also showed us the two garages that housed various garden tools.

We walked back up the hill towards the car, and I stopped and looked around. I just couldn't get enough of the sight: the acres and acres of green, green grass; the stately trees; the waterfall; the . . . it was just too perfect to believe.

I breathed in that clean country air in gulps. With good reason — I hadn't yet asked how much it all cost! I was afraid, but I had to find out.

"Sir, how much are they asking for this place?" I asked. There was a long pause.

"Here it comes," I thought. My heart was pounding.

"I'm sorry, I don't know," he answered. "You'll have to talk to the man who runs the place. He won't be back until tomorrow evening."

Elsie and I were pretty letdown as we headed back to Brooklyn. We were sure the place was way out of our reach.

The next day I called the owner. The price was $225,000, fully furnished. No, it wasn't a million dollars as I had thought it might be. But it might as well have been! Where could we ever raise that amount? We had decided that $100,000 was absolutely tops.

When I told Dave the price, he didn't act shocked; he just said he thought they'd sell for much less. He and I drove up to Garrison a few days later and took a complete tour. Dave was very impressed. When we got down by the stream and the swimming pool, he said he felt this was the place God wanted us to buy.

"John, let's have a word of prayer. Let's believe that God is going to give us this place for the girls," Dave said.

I'm certainly in favor of prayer, but would God really provide a place like this for us? It was more than we could possibly afford. Yet, if God wanted us to have it, He would work miracles for us to get it.

"That's a good idea," I said.

Then Dave prayed. And when Dave prays, he makes a very direct and specific prayer — no flowery words; he just claimed this property for Him.

When we got back to the Center in Brooklyn, that afternoon, I called the union that owned the estate and made an appointment with the appropriate people. The following day, Dave and I went over to see them. During the negotiations, they brought the price down to $175,000. (A real estate agent wasn't involved, so we had that advantage.) We told the officers of the union that we had only $20,000 for a down payment, and after a brief discussion, they said they would take it. They owned the property outright, and they were willing to carry the mortgage. We would pay $10,000 a year as a mortgage payment, plus interest. The first year's total payment of mortgage and interest would be around $19,910. It was due next December 31st, but Dave and I had a couple of ideas as to where we might dig up the money for that first payment.

We signed the papers!

What a time we had moving up there — from the hell of Brooklyn to the heaven of Garrison! The staff and the girls were beside themselves with excitement. We all kept praising the Lord for His wonderful provision. Finally, we had a home for our girls; and, in addition, God had provided a place for teenage camping.

That summer we had a great time with teenage camping. A couple of weeks we had so many girls, they had to double up — two to a bed. But these girls didn't mind. Don't forget they were coming from the hot, steaming jungle of the ghetto to this pleasant, cool haven. I wish you could have been there to see the expressions on their faces, as they enjoyed the wonderful facilities God had provided.

One day I was on the side of the hill mowing the grass. The mower broke down, and I was busy trying to repair it, when two of our teenage girls came walking along the pathway, below me. They didn't know I was there, but I heard their conversation.

One girl said, "Man, when I get back to the city, I'm sure not gonna do the things I used to do."

This from a girl who when she had come to us had smoked marijuana, and whose family had been greatly concerned over her belligerence and unruliness! Christ had really changed her life that week.

About a month later this girl was at one of our Saturday-night rallies in Brooklyn. She had brought a friend and, at the close of the service, her girlfriend went forward to receive Christ. What a beautiful sight — to see both of them kneeling at the altar! Today, after many months, this young girl is serving Christ. No longer does she use marijuana or hang out with the wrong crowd; she has become a fine, Christian young lady.

It was so much easier now to have girls come from the city. We still had problems, of course, when they kicked their habits; but at least here they were not so close to the subway. When they came up here, they stayed longer. Down in Brooklyn we could provide for only thirteen girls, but that summer we had nineteen at one time.

When September came, we were fortunate enough to send eleven of them off to Bible School and to fill their empty beds with other girls seeking help.

The months flew by, and December came. On December fifth I suddenly realized I had to have $10,000 by December 31st. The idea we'd had originally, concerning the mortgage money, had collapsed. I was stuck and concerned as to where the money would come from. I was led by the Lord to go back to the Jones Foundation to speak to Mr. Farrell, hoping they would give again, as they had when they gave us the $15,000 for the Girl's Home.

Our excellent staff photographer, Bob Combs, came up to Garrison and took pictures of our facilities and our girls. He took pictures and pictures and pictures: of girls in our home; of our teen-girl summer camping program; of the dining hall; of the stream . . . Bob made up a beautiful album which I planned to give to Mr. Farrell.

I presented the album to him, as a token of our appreciation, when I met him in his office on Wall Street. Mr. Farrell seemed quite pleased and inquired about the purchase of the estate. I told him all about it and asked if the Foundation could help us out, once again.

"Well, Reverend Benton, you know we can't give again this year because we already gave $15,000 in the Spring," Mr. Farrell said.

I knew it was rare for a Foundation to give twice in one year, But I had hopes. I was pretty glum, but I kept hoping God would work another miracle.

"I'll tell you what, though, let me look here at my calendar," Mr. Farrell said.

He leafed through his calendar and said, "December 31st is on a Sunday. Monday, the 1st of January, is a holiday. If I sent you $15,000 on the second, you would get it on Wednesday, the 3rd. How would that be?"

I almost shouted "Hallelujah" aloud. Dignity kept it in my heart, but I am sure that God heard it!

"Oh, Mr. Farrell, you have no idea how much we appreciate that," I said. "Praise the Lord!"

The burden and strain of financing our home slipped from my shoulders.

"Miss Quinn, could you come here for a minute, please?" Mr. Farrell called.

Mr. Farrell introduced me to Miss Quinn, his secretary, and began to dictate: "Miss Quinn, take this note for me. The Walter Hoving Home has purchased the former estate of Local 32B for the sum of $175,000. $20,000 has been paid down and a balance of $155,000 is to be paid by the Jones Foundation, at $15,000 a year until the balance is paid off."

I could hardly believe my ears " . . . the balance of $155,000 to be paid by the Jones Foundation, at $15,000 a year until the balance is paid off."

Tears welled in my eyes as I thought how good God was to us!

I tried my best to thank Mr. Farrell, but words were difficult to find. Mr. Farrell just smiled. He is such a gentleman.

I have never met Mrs. Jones of the Jones Foundation, but her generosity and that of her late husband has determined the future of hundreds of needy girls.

If it hadn't been for the kindness of Mrs. Jones and Mr. Farrell, Christ would have never been able to change the lives of all these girls. Many of them might have died from overdoses, been murdered by perverted individuals, or wound up in jail. May God abundantly bless these two for their generosity.

We have been here more than 25 years and have since built more buildings on the property.

I never get tired of driving up that long driveway past the two stone pillars. I still have vivid memories of those chaotic days in Brooklyn, and the contrast is so satisfying.

Yes, it does take just as much faith to believe God for a leaky tent as it does for a huge cathedral!

You see, I have been forced to live by faith. And let me tell you from experience, it's a tough way to live.

It seems that in this ministry we are always living on the edge, never having enough money to do what God has called us to do.

After almost 20 years in Garrison, Elsie and decided to launch another venture of faith.

We went to Pasadena to establish another Walte Hoving Home.

California has some very strict zoning laws, and we weren't able to get a large estate like the one in Garrison.

But we did get comfortable and adequate homes

The first Home was large enough for six girls

Then we got the home next door and increased our population to fifteen ladies.

Elsie and I are still in charge of both ministries — Garrison, New York and Pasadena, California. We go back and forth every month and continue to thrive on the ministry of the streets and jails.

Thousands of ladies have come to Christ because He provided these homes for us.

But it has not been easy. In fact, it got so bad we went right to the edge. We were going to have to make the awful decision of shutting down the homes. I just couldn't bring myself to do it, even though people were demanding that they be paid.

It was one of the worst times of my life.

CHAPTER 9
PUSHED TO THE EDGE OF DESPAIR

I couldn't take one more telephone call.

It was frustrating, embarrassing, and I just couldn't handle it. Everybody wanted their money, and I had no money to pay them.

The ministry had gotten to the place where it was facing bankruptcy. We just didn't have enough income to pay all our bills.

Up until that last telephone call I had tried my very best to solve the problem.

One of the quickest ways is to cut expenses. And we did that.

Because the Garrison estate is so large, we had three maintenance men. I had to let two of them go.

We embarked on a very ambitious cost-saving program. We got the girls and staff together and figured out where every penny was going.

It still wasn't enough. I had to cut back some more.

The cook was the next one we let go. When I mentioned that to the staff, everybody was concerned what we would do next.

I told the staff, "We'll just have to have the girls do the cooking."

You should have been there when I said that. It was like the staff came unglued. They yelled at me! "We can't have the girls cooking. Can you imagine what will happen in that kitchen? There are big butcher knives! The first argument those girls have, someone is going to get stabbed to death."

I thought about that. They did have a point. What would happen if these girls who had been gang members had an argument in the kitchen?

But I knew it was either cut expenses or shut down the ministry. I think I'd almost have quit first and let someone else handle that problem.

I told the staff, "If the girls kill themselves, they kill themselves. We've got to cut back."

I then asked Elsie if she would begin to train the ladies how to cook. And then a wonderful thing happened.

Since the girls helped plan the menu and cook the meals, there was a great amount of enthusiasm for the new responsibility!

In fact, to encourage the girls, after the meal was served, everyone would applaud for the cooks. With that kind of treatment the cooks had a great feeling of accomplishment.

To this day we still do that. I've often thought what would happen in families if the father and children gave a big round of applause for Mom when she cooked a good meal?

We never criticize the girls. Though they may sometimes burn the toast or put too much seasoning in the food, we still clap.

With all the cost-cutting, we still did not solve the problem.

The telephone calls continued. It was so embarrassing to me as a Christian to try to answer these people. They had to pay their bills, too. Furthermore, I had a great sense of guilt. This was not the way a Christian should be acting. We had obligations, and I believe it was our Christian responsibility to pay them. But we had no money.

I counted up the bills we had to pay. They came to $11,000.

In those days that was an enormous amount. Our ministries have grown since then, but at that time, $11,000 was an unreachable goal. I suppose it would be like $100,000 today.

At that time I was serving on the Board of Directors of the Teen Challenge Training Center in Pennsylvania. (The boys' part of the Teen Challenge ministry.)

The following morning I had to get up very early and drive for about four hours to make a 9:00 o'clock board meeting.

That meant I had to leave at 5:00 o'clock in the morning. But those four hours were times I could spend alone with the Lord.

As I drove down there I frantically began to seek God for the answer to our financial dilemma.

As I poured out my heart to God, I began to sob over this critical problem. Bankruptcy would be a tragic way to end the ministry.

I knew about other ministries having to close due to lack of finances. I wondered if we would soon be numbered among them.

With tears streaming down my face, I pleaded with the Lord for help. I asked the Holy Spirit what to do.

That wonderful still, small voice spoke to me again. The Lord said, "Write a letter to the people. Tell them exactly what you have done and ask them to help you with the $11,000 financial crisis."

The next day, back in my office, I sat down and dictated the letter I felt the Lord wanted me to write.

I told the people on our mailing list of the financial crisis we were facing. I also let them know we had cut back on staff, pared expenses to the very bone, but we were still losing the battle and needed $11,000.

Joyce, our business manager, and I prayed over the letter and we sent it to our mailing list.

Would you believe that one of the first responses we got to the letter was a check for $11,000!

It came from Lila Wallace. Lila and her husband, DeWitt Wallace, were the owners of Readers Digest.

For the life of me, I don't know how my "junk mail" type of letter got to her. Lila and her husband were known for their giving, and I am sure everybody in the country had sent letters to them. I'm sure they received letters by the truckloads from people with worthwhile causes asking them for help.

Mrs. Wallace sent just a short note. She believed these were the days when charitable organizations needed to cut back, and because of what we had done, she wanted to help us with the problem.

There sat the check for $11,000.

When we opened the mail, I was so excited I almost jumped out the third floor of the building where our offices were. God had answered!

Other people responded, and we were able to pay our bills. God was faithful.

I kept wondering why God had answered this way. It was a mystery to me.

Down the hall, in the bookkeeper's office, was a check for $5 and a handwritten note. I could tell the note was from an older lady by the way she wrote.

I went back down the hall and sat in my office chair. I began praying to the Lord and asking him why people had responded so generously.

Now mind you, I was praying with that letter in my

hand. What I have to say next you may not understand.

Just as I completed that prayer, I felt God's Spirit come out of that letter and start up my arm. The hairs on my arm stood straight out. It was a strong, tingling sensation. I kid you not, this is what happened.

And then the Holy Spirit spoke to me, "The reason I answered the way I did is because the anointing of the Spirit of God was on those letters."

I learned one of the greatest lessons of my Christian life. It takes the anointing of God to accomplish His work here in this world. Since that time, I have always prayed over every letter I have sent out when I have asked for finances. I honestly believe the Holy Spirit speaks to people when they read our appeal letters. And, thank God, many people have responded to the voice of the Lord and have helped us out.

Let me tell you about another significant event that has happened in the ministry of the Walter Hoving Home.

While Mr. Hoving was still its chairman, Tiffany & Company manufactured the TRY GOD pin.

It's an interesting story how this all came about.

Mr. Hoving was a member of a church on Park Avenue. The woman who ran the kitchen there was vitally concerned about the problems America was facing.

She told Mr. Hoving, "Tiffany's needs to make a pin that says Try God. We've tried everything else in this world to solve our problems, but now it's time to try God."

Mr. Hoving didn't pay much attention to what the woman was trying to tell him. He heard all kinds of ideas on what Tiffany's should do. They are essentially in the jewelry business and things of that nature, and really weren't in the business of manufacturing religious pins.

But the woman kept after him. She tried to convince Mr. Hoving that not only would it be a great pin, but a wonderful way to spread a simple message to the world: to try God.

The woman would not give up. Mr. Hoving finally relented and told her Tiffany's would at least try it. Then he went to talk to his designers.

I shall never forget when Mr. Hoving presented the idea at a meeting of the Walter Hoving Home Advisory Board. All of us got very excited.

Mr. Hoving wasn't very enthusiastic. He said, "I tell you what we are going to do. We will make a thousand of these pins. If they don't sell, we'll just ship them up to the Walter Hoving Home and you can do what you want with them."

Mr. Hoving put an advertisement in the New York Times paper about the pins. He mentioned our ministry. The profit would go to the Home.

And then Tiffany's waited to see if anybody would buy one of those pins. To say the least, it was most unusual for Tiffany's to do this.

The New York Times paper is not only sold in New York City and the greater New York area, but in different cities around the United States.

Tiffany's has a store in Los Angeles. When the people in Los Angeles got the New York Times, they went into the Los Angeles Tiffany's to buy the TRY GOD pin.

Of course the sales people knew nothing about it. In fact, they were actually quite amused that someone would think of something like this.

The manager called New York and asked about it. Yes, there was a TRY GOD pin and they had advertised it.

That day Tiffany's in New York sold out their TRY GOD pins!

It was a very profitable venture for Mr. Hoving. In fact, Billy Graham even used TRY GOD pins to help finance some of his television crusades. Many of us greatly benefitted from this.

And the profits during those days greatly helped to expand our ministry in Garrison.

All of us wore our TRY GOD pin very proudly. To this day, I occasionally run into people who still have one of those pins. It has been a blessing in many ways.

Speaking of Mr. Hoving, he was a godsend to this ministry from the very beginning.

For a number of years we had our board meetings at Tiffany's, which was always a great event.

When he passed away it was a great loss to all of us. He was a godly man of great wisdom. All of us admired him. Our loss is certainly heaven's gain.

A few have asked if Mr. Hoving endowed the Home when he passed away. There was no endowment setup. We are carrying on without him, but he was mightily used of God to establish the ministry.

The whole life of the Walter Hoving Home has been one miracle after another.

We still need money. We always have. We are a ministry, not a business. We make no profit other than seeing ladies who are addicts and prostitutes being transformed by the power of Christ.

The reason we don't have money is that what we receive we spend and invest in the lives of others. And I suppose that is the way we will always be.

And it is because of dear friends like you that we are able to keep these doors open to so many girls in New York and California.

Today it still takes the miraculous power of God to do what he has called us to do.

I wish I could tell you the names of two sisters, but they want to remain anonymous and I respect their wishes. However, they have played a very significant role in this ministry.

And not only in this ministry. They don't know it, but they were the means the Holy Spirit used to help our family out of a very difficult situation.

Before I get back to these two special ladies, let me tell you how this all came about.

After we had moved from Brooklyn up to Garrison, Elsie, our three children and I lived on the second floor of the main building with all the rest of the girls in the program. We had our own three bedrooms, and that was just about it.

When we first started the ministry, Elsie and I made a decision that we would always involve our children in it.

However, when we moved to Brooklyn, we knew we were in trouble. It was a very dangerous area, and trying to raise three white children in a minority neighborhood was going to be tough. In fact, one of Elsie's sisters even offered to have our children move in with her. She was concerned that something terrible would happen to them.

Being new to the ministry, we did not know what kind of input these girls from the street could have on our children's lives. Ladies who had many years of crime, prostitution, and whatever, might have a very negative effect on them.

Especially on our son, Jim. At the time he was five

years old. Growing up in that environment, no one could predict what would happen to him.

But our three children, Marji, Connie and Jim got involved with us in ministry. Our oldest daughter, Marji, used to go out on the streets with me. Connie, our second daughter, would always pray for girls who were kicking their drug habit cold turkey. And Jim was a little brother to the girls.

We were certainly blessed by God to move out of that terrible environment and into the country. But our problems did not stop there.

Elsie and I were having some personal problems. We couldn't seem to get along together. Looking back, I realize it was the pressure of the ministry and not being able to maintain our privacy in the main house.

Our bedroom was next to the "kicking room," and in the night we could sometimes hear the painful cries of the ladies kicking their dope habit. To say the least, it was intense. The whole situation was really getting to us.

I discussed this problem with my good friend David Wilkerson, and he suggested we move out of the main house. That was not going to be very easy; there simply was no place to move into.

At that time we were trying to put aside money to build an additional dormitory for more girls. We were crowded, and it was tough turning ladies down because we had no room.

I told Dave about this money we were putting aside. Dave said he felt the Lord wanted us to use that money to build us a home on the property. I objected.

I tried to explain to Dave that I felt we should provide for the girls first. After we built the additional girls' home, we could go ahead and build a place for us.

But Dave is a man of great wisdom. He said, "John, put your family first and God will take care of that additional girls' home."

So we built a simple three-bedroom home about a hundred feet away from the main house.

And a very strange thing happened. When I moved into that house I was depressed for three days! I really should have been thanking God for our new home, but it was a real change from being right in the middle of the action all the time.

Thank God, I got over it. Elsie, the kids and I were able to feel like a family again. We still kept busy and as active as ever in the ministry with the girls, but we now had a restful haven to call home.

It was after we had moved into our home that the two sisters came into our lives.

One of the sisters had sent a donation, and I called to thank her for what she had done.

A short time later I had the privilege of visiting with

her in her home. Because of that first contact she and her sister came to visit us at the Walter Hoving Home.

While they were up in Garrison with us, I shared with them the burden of trying to build an additional girls' home. At that time I did not know God was fulfilling what Dave Wilkerson had told me: put my family first, and God would supply the money for the additional girls home.

Elsie and I took the ladies back to their home. Shortly after that one of the sisters called me to visit with her again.

When I got to her place she shared with me her concern for our ministry.

As we discussed the additional girls' home I told her I thought it would cost something over $100,000.

She then told me she was donating some stock and that stock was later sold for $120,000.

I can't tell you the joy I had when she told me that!

And the miracle continued.

We started building the home. As we got near its completion, it was going to cost us $140,000 rather than $120.000.

I wrote back to the lady, sharing this problem with her. Bless her dear heart, she in turn, sent a check for $20,000 to complete the building.

That was many years ago. Today, both the ladies,

who are up in years, continue to be two saints of God. They have helped with other projects through the years and have become a vital part of all that has been done in this ministry.

The Bible talks about angels visiting us unaware. I sometimes think both sisters are God's special angels to this ministry.

For many years Elsie and I enjoyed the blessing of our home on the campus. Marji, Connie and Jim grew and went through school, and eventually all three got married.

Today they and their families are all serving the Lord, along with our eight grandchildren.

Marji and her husband Dave and their two boys, Joshua and Adam, worked for us for eleven years.

Connie and her husband, Rick, and their three children Brooke, Will and Eric, are missionaries in Holland.

Our son Jim, his wife Judy, and their children Jayme, Jarrett and Julee, are directors of the Teen Challenge girls home in Springfield, Missouri. Jim worked for us for five years in Garrison. What he learned he used to build a very successful program in Springfield.

Jim and I get along very well as father and son. I have great respect for what he is doing. He was asked why he left the Walter Hoving Home in Garrison and he told one of my board members, "I've taught my

Dad all he could possibly know in five years, so I felt it was time to move on." That's my son Jim!

I want to tell you about one young lady who was probably the greatest miracle we've ever experienced. Though every lady is a miracle, this one was so unusual.

When Tina walked through our front door for help, I couldn't believe what I was confronting.

I looked into Tina's eyes and they were glazed. Her hair was frizzed straight out, as though she had put her fingers in a socket.

Her arm was in a sling.

When I looked at her, I knew we couldn't help her. I tried to talk to her and she couldn't complete a sentence.

I knew she was too far gone for the Walter Hoving Home to help her.

But God had other plans.

CHAPTER 10
THE GREATEST MIRACLE

They told me Tina not only had a severe problem of drug addiction, but other things were bothering her. When she closed her eyes she could see evil spirits. And when it was quiet she heard their voices.

I knew what was the matter with her. She was severely emotionally disturbed. I thought she might be demon-possessed too.

By this time we had developed a well-structured program. Our ladies get up at 6:00 a.m. to pray for an hour. After breakfast we have a time of prayer around the tables. Then, after cleanup, the girls go to school.

Because the girls come from varied backgrounds we have an individualized learning program that's specifically adapted to each particular girl. While they're here they take 52 subjects, all of which are Bible-based and life-changing. Such subjects as You Can Become A Somebody Again, Soul Winning, God Works Miracles, Establishing Priorities, When Does Growth Really Start, Getting Along With People, Managing Your Moods, Overcoming Fear, How to Face Your Failures, How A Christian Woman Can Become Useful, Self Control.

I wish I had the opportunity to list all the subjects.

They are just fantastic!

These many subjects help our ladies become women of God. In addition to this, Tina would be involved in group lessons, where she would get to interact with others.

Unfortunately, as much as we have tried, we've never been able to help a severely emotionally disturbed person. God only knows how hard we've tried. In fact, one time we took one in and she went berserk. She went to the kitchen, grabbed a huge butcher knife, and tried to murder two of our staff.

I was right in the middle of that fracas. I was terribly afraid that we would never make it. But thank God, we got out of that one. Though we had to call the police, nobody got killed.

And I knew Tina had the same potential.

At an early age Tina had been repeatedly molested. You can't imagine the harmful effect incest has on children. Their outlook on life becomes terribly warped and they lose all sense of dignity and purpose.

Tina was also a twin. Unfortunately, her family accepted her sister and not Tina. To get rid of the terrible pain of rejection in the family, Tina turned to an alternative. It was drugs.

She found her greatest release in taking the drug, acid. Like PCP and other similar drugs, acid is worse than heroin or cocaine. It can damage the mind beyond repair.

You might have heard the term, "an addict's brains are fried." I've seen those advertisements on television with fried eggs. What really happens is, the brain heats up. Through that intense heat, brain matter is destroyed.

Though there was rejection in Tina's family, they spent lots of money trying to cure her of her drug addiction.

They took her to the best doctors and hospitals, but nothing seemed to help Tina give up her drugs.

She said, "When I'm high nothing matters. It doesn't make any difference about the problems of incest. Or rejection. Being high destroys those problems, and I live in utopia. That's why I keep getting high."

Tina told me one time she'd gotten high with a group of people. Something happened and she passed out. When she came to, she was in the woods someplace. Her face was down in the mud, as it had been raining. Then she looked at her body. She had no clothes on.

Later on Tina would find out what had happened. While she was passed out, she had been raped. She didn't know who it was or how many times.

She got to her feet in the woods and staggered to a farm house. They put a coat around her and called the police.

They followed standard procedure for someone in

115

Tina's condition. They put her in a mental institution.

By this time, Tina's condition had so deteriorated that they had tried everything to cure her.

They even gave Tina shock treatments. Over 30 of them. At that time shock therapy was used to cure drug addicts. I've never met one who has been cured by that therapy, but I've met some who have almost had their lives destroyed by that terrible approach. Like Tina.

Tina kept going in and out of mental institutions. She was severely suicidal. While in the mental institution, she became violent.

Because of seeing evil spirits when she had her eyes closed, she would try to pluck her eyeballs out of their sockets. To stop the voices she kept banging her head against the wall.

The hospital staff had only one choice. They put her in solitary confinement.

In this particular hospital, that meant she was placed in a cell in the basement. The floors, walls, and ceiling were padded, and they stripped her of all her clothing.

Tina sat in that cell stark naked, with no one to talk to and no one to help her.

Periodically they would come in and check on her. Because of her horrible physical and mental condition, Tina would cower in the corner. Hunched together in the fetal position, she'd rock back and forth.

The conditions were beyond description. Tina said that when it came time for a shock treatment, she could hear the gurney coming down the hall. As soon as she heard it, she would cringe. Shock treatments would knock you unconscious; the pain was unbearable.

The orderlies would unlock Tina's cell door, and grab her and throw her on the gurney. Then they would strap her down. All this time she didn't have any clothes on.

She felt worse than an animal. If only she could die!

Tina tried many times to kill herself. She said she was even a failure at that. She couldn't kill herself and end it all.

After the numerous shock treatments Tina got no better. In fact, she got worse.

The psychiatrist came to visit Tina in her cell one day. She was all huddled up, and he kicked her in the ribs.

This psychiatrist said, "Tina, you've just got to get use to it. There's no hope for you."

Something exploded inside Tina. She knew there was no hope for her. No hope. Never, ever any hope.

The thought raced through her mind: "There's no

hope for me. There's no hope for me."

If only she could die, but she couldn't even do that.

One Sunday afternoon a Christian lady came to the institution. She inquired about the girl in the padded cell. The nurse told her that was Tina, and tried to explain to this Christian woman that there was no hope for her.

The woman asked if she could see Tina. And talk to her. The nurse said Tina was violent and could not communicate.

Then the Christian lady said, "Could I just read to her from the Bible?"

The lady persisted. Finally the nurse relented and said, "We'll let you in. But you're going to be locked in. Tina is a violent person, and if anything happens to you it's your fault."

The Christian woman was not deterred. She knew the power of the gospel of Christ.

When they opened the cell door this dear woman could not believe what she saw. But no matter, she knew that a person could not plunge beyond the grasp of Jesus.

The woman tried to communicate, but there was nothing from Tina. So she sat down and began to read the Word of God to Tina.

Tina did not respond. But the woman would not give up.

She came back the next week and the next.

Finally Tina began to have just a little response.

After some time, the hospital decided to release Tina. And she ended up here at the Walter Hoving Home!

So now Tina stood in our front room. But I knew we couldn't help her. She was too far gone.

We discussed Tina with our program administrator. The program administrator felt we could help her. But I had my doubts.

I finally decided to try it. But we agreed we'd only do it one day at a time. I certainly did not want to have another girl going berserk and not be able to handle a violent situation.

Tina started into our program. She had great difficulty. She still couldn't complete her sentences, and memorizing scripture was very difficult. But she wouldn't give up.

It took her three weeks to memorize Luke 1:37: "For with God nothing shall be impossible."

Tina grasped that and began to ask Jesus to change her life.

When she closed her eyes she still saw those evil spirits, so she learned to pray with her eyes open.

Tina kept on in the program. She would not give up.

I believe in demons, and I have actually seen one.

I know about people exorcising demon-possessed people. But in Tina's case, her deliverance did not come this way.

I honestly believe it was the entrance of God's Word that drove out the demonic power. Tina doesn't know the exact date it happened, but somewhere in the next few months the spirits left her. She didn't see them any more. And the voices stopped.

Even while Tina was in the hospital and had reached her lowest point, she says there was another voice that spoke to her and said, "There is hope."

I knew whose voice that was. That was the voice of the Lord.

Tina stayed with us and completed the program. We encouraged her to go on to college.

She did go to college and graduated with a 3.5 grade point average.

Tina helped launch the program in California. She went on to graduate school. There she got a 4.0 average.

Today, Tina is an outstanding Christian with a wonderful husband. She serves on three State Legislative Committees for mental health and is a real professional as well as a great Christian.

To me Tina represents what the Walter Hoving Home is all about. We do believe Christ can change the life of a person who puts her faith in Him.

As I look at the problem of drug addiction and prostitution it absolutely overwhelms me.

And it is getting worse.

But the Lord has brought the Walter Hoving Home into being.

Elsie and I have dedicated ourselves, for the rest of our lives, to go out to the streets and prisons and rescue these girls.

Unfortunately, we can't do it alone.

I pray, as you have been able to share in the experience and the ministry of the Walter Hoving Home, that you have caught the burden to reach these lost girls.

Every day at the Walter Hoving Home in Garrison, New York, as well as Pasadena, California, we continue to see miracles taking place.

Ladies who have an unbelievable past — years of prostitution, drug addiction, horrible incest, rejection by family — are now restored by the power of Christ.

That's what we are all about.

Even though Elsie and I continue to face many dangers in the ministry, girls like Tina and thousands of others keep telling us every day . . . just keep on saving one lady at a time.

Since 1967, thousands of young women have found new life and new hope at the Walter Hoving Home. The Walter Hoving Home is nationally recognized for the high cure rate among the alcoholic and drug-addicted women who complete its spiritually-oriented rehabilitation program as alcoholics, drug addicts and prostitutes have found a happy, healthy way of living through the power of Christ. The success of the program is made possible through the prayers and support of individuals who are committed to helping young ladies gain freedom from the bondage of drugs, alcohol, and prostitution. Will you help us in this work by sending a gift today?

Walter Hoving Home
P.O. Box 194
Garrison, New York 10524
(914) 424-3674

or

Walter Hoving Home
P.O. Box 94304
Pasadena, California 91109
(626) 405-0950

Your Gift will help save "One Lady at a Time."

The Walter Hoving Home depends upon the contributions of friends like you to help cover the costs of caring for the hundreds of young women who come to the facility in New York and California. At our residential rehabilitation program, we provide food, shelter, clothing, medical care, educational and vocational training as well as spiritual guidance and Christian teaching. If you can, please send a gift to help an abused and neglected lady find new life.

YES! I will help you rescue young ladies through the Walter Hoving Home. I'm enclosing my gift of:

$10_____ $20 _____ $50 _____ Other _____

Name _____

Address _____

City_____ St. _____

Zip _____

Please make your check payable to the Walter Hoving Home. Your gift is tax deductable.

Walter Hoving Home
P.O. Box 94304, Pasadena, California 91109

or

Walter Hoving Home
P.O. Box 194, Garrison, New York 10524